T0253054

POLKADOT WOUNDS

Anthony Vahni Capildeo FRSL is a Trinidadian Scottish writer of poetry and non-fiction. Currently Professor and Writer in Residence at the University of York, their site-specific word and visual art includes responses to Cornwall's former capital, Launceston, as the Causley Trust Poet in Residence (2022) and to the Ubatuba granite of the Henry Moore Institute in Leeds (2023), as well as to Scottish, Irish, and Caribbean built and natural environments. Their numerous books and pamphlets, from *No Traveller Returns* (Salt, 2003), *Person Animal Figure* (Landfill, 2005) onwards, are distinguished by deliberate engagement with independent and small presses. Their work has been recognized with the Cholmondeley Award (Society of Authors) and the Forward Poetry Prize for Best Collection. Their publications include *Like a Tree, Walking* (Carcanet, 2021) (Poetry Book Society Choice), and A Happiness (Intergraphia, 2022). Their interests include silence, translation theory, medieval reworkings, plurilingualism, collaborative work, and traditional masquerade. Recent commissions include research-based Windrush poems for Poet in the City and for the Royal Society of Literature. Capildeo served as a judge for the Jhalak Prize (2023).

CARCANET POETRY

Polkadot Wounds
Anthony Vahni Capildeo

First published in Great Britain in 2024 by
Carcanet
Alliance House, 30 Cross Street
Manchester, M 2 7 A Q
www.carcanet.co.uk

Text copyright © Anthony Vahni Capildeo 2024

The right of Anthony Vahni Capildeo to be identified as the author
of this work has been asserted in accordance with the
Copyright, Design and Patents Act of 1988; all rights reserved.

A CIP catalogue record for this book is
available from the British Library.

ISBN 978 1 80017 425 2

Book design by Andrew Latimer, Carcanet
Typesetting by LiteBook Prepress Services
Printed in Great Britain by SRP Ltd, Exeter, Devon

The publisher acknowledges financial
assistance from Arts Council England.

CONTENTS

GENTLE HOUSEWORK OF THE SACRIFICE

for Katie Grant

POLKADOT WOUNDS

SUMMER, LAUNCESTON
St Cuthbert Mayne

WHERE STONE RUNS ◊ LIKE
HONEY ◊ BECAUSE THE SEA ◊
IS A TYPE OF ◊ DESERT ◊
SPINE ◊ OF SELF-STRIPPING THORNS
◊ NOW BEING RUINED ◊
WARMING TO YOU ◊ I LET IN
THE ◊ LIGHT ◊ ◊ ◊ YOU ROSE
STEM ◊ LONG AGO, NEWLY ◊
DEAD AND ◊ RISEN ◊ ◊ ◊
TREASURE WHAT YOU ◊ SAY
◊ BECAUSE ◊ NOBODY'S REAL
FACE EXISTS ◊ YET ◊ POLKADOT
WOUNDS ◊ WHERE STONE ◊ RUNS
◊ LIKE HONEY ◊ ◊ ◊ ◊ ◊

LANDSKIPS

VISIT
for K.M. Grant

the house of the inventors
of rainfall's calibration
hidden rooms steadying kindest rooms
livability above secrecy
celebration singing
that way stone halls
Jacobean flooring empty armour
love there are times
you'd lose your head
so many in conversation
woodgrain with buttered
dna with waveform

come away a little
visit the house
of musicians' comforting
pleasecomeflying patterns
invitations to lyric
meanwhile moor
on the edge
welcome also ferrets
eager-eyed though of unpleasing reputation
wreathing wearable greetings
shy and sharp-toothed
wristwarmer endearments

the bees' balsam
honey of the fields
too intense their wargames
too far up the hill
surpassing sweet

too thin
bring a black queen from Ireland
bring never send
no never send back
refund the beekeeper
for the bees' behaviour
suggestion such gestion

come come down
from grey horseheight
come in from the white horse's mane
stream into the garden
myrtle amethyst
yew rose and thyme
hidden rooms steadying kindest rooms
the house of the inventors
of rainfall's calibration
expanding light hours
round a living dream
so many in conversation

FULL-CIRCLE BELLS
for Leila Capildeo

Mama, I'm swimming down three flights of stairs
in green light. You can't hear me yet. The tree
I'm walking past has put on ocean airs.
Up two more flights, I can't hear for the bells
cathedralling connexion: visible
to invisible world, embrace! The box

sits blackly on the landing wall. *Ayyy*, box,
you're too high up! A gecko on the stairs,
my body stretches, flattens, visible
to students who 'go home', not 'phone home'. Tree
doesn't sound submarine to them; no bells,
no whistles, hum and buzz, press on their airs.

No bloody privacy. So, put on airs
they can't translate. *Hola, dígame*, box,
can I get home on this line? Riding bells,
the idea of earthquakes shatters up the stairs.
Whales dive, chew through cable. Windstruck, a tree
snaps wires. Numbers make you visible,

I dial them, the dirt ain't visible,
but grotty to my fingerpads. Coined airs
join bells, *hojas rojas* singe the frosty tree,
I flatten like a gecko to the box
for a collect call, *Dios, cuántas* stairs,
AMERICAS-1 SOUTH, submarine cable, bells.

Drink purpling Virginia creeper. Bells
are more than bread. *Mira* what's visible
till it compounds and vanishes: your stairs
are an island, full of twangling airs.
Sway and speak your heart into a box,
your mother's voice is leafing like a tree

while leaves are falling from the ocean tree
you must pass on the way to bells
that tick five hours apart. A telephone box
is a time zone box. You're a visible
time traveller – but give yourself no airs,
chiquita, there're drunk rowers on the stairs.

1990s, Victorian stairs,
your voice held in my hand, mine thinned by airs,
my dusk your noon, only the timebox visible.

WEATHER SYSTEMS
for Caroline Bergvall

Where is the wind in the time before dawn?
Gathering fast on a straight course to storm.

Where is the wind in the reddening day?
Colder than mountains that would break its way.

Where is the wind when the morning bell rings?
Stilling the satellite's eye with its rings.

Where is the wind in the white masque of noon?
Hiding a power it shadows forth soon.

Where is the wind when the children leave school?
Gathering force on a swift course to rule.

Where is the wind when the helpless one prays?
Filling with dust that Sahara winds raise.

How does this wind cope with desert winds' burden?
Badly; and suddenly slower, uncertain.

What shall we do now we're saved from the storm?
Breathe dust-reddened air and wake before dawn.

*

anocht at night tonight it knocks
on the roof í nótt knocks gallops
last night anoche would it last
or cave in the roof would it last
night knocking and galloping nox
perpetually drumming on

*

Where may they find you, Caroline?
Danger to life is forecast,
My friend gone out, singing back to the wind.

Your words a stand of cherry trees.
My spring cued by technicians.
It is my turn to go, your singing bird.

You were their director, lighthouse.
Now breaking on other waves,
The beams you send out strive towards what strand.

We were alive before the plague,
Alive in one place, many
Alive in one piece; we were alive, Caroline

Who has been France, Norway, memory,
Dreams of a non-lethal crowd
Baptized and crowned in bright and lisping haar.

Let them give you the microphone,
Bring the big screen, Caroline.
Show us night by erasures, dawn again.

*

The sun is a girl in the north and a man in high boots in the
east and a vicious blond in the betweenlands.

The king's perfume is roses to the west and amber to the east
and further west the kings are whaleshit or raw.

The bridegroom wears pink in my land and drinks apricot
brandy in another land and often arrives on a white horse.

I know the girl who makes the man stoop to drink milk she
pours into mud, and how she feels great.

I know the man who confused a girl with a pearl, purity with
an irritable secretion, the moon that fails with a quarry, a
witch, peace lacking in justice.

I know the wolf who is monogamous, and I who am ivory
and microplastics in the making, and numerous hesitancies
that flee and swagger in the surface of a river picked up by
the tail.

*

when day breaks
it will not be mended with gold,
it will be infinitely more
precious, and perhaps survivable.

If you're thinking ahead don't
do that, you're on the island now.
going full Bofin
Giving away whatever you brought to sell.
　　　The clocks at Murray's are inverted.
going deep Bofin
It makes a difference. It makes
sense. We'll figure it out
Deirdre says, imagine if everyone
who came to the island
took away a stone from the island?
Extreme & scattering
bright…
　　　I pick out my spot in the cemetery;
Fever & general shutdown.
Gabrielle opens a red bag & gives me good pills.
　　　Elaine can do the dead man's float forever,
Pauline likes blue cheese,
the lady in the craft caravan has gone
vegan, changing our three-year conversation
about fudge. I buy a fairy door for Alex.
I know Noel's house mostly
by the hidden corncrake.
I sleep there in the attic; Anne-Sofia pencil-sketches
the invisible corncrake.
on the island now
extreme Bofin
Crex crex, scattering bright…
　　　Alan the novelist is made to hear
who has rapey exes; he listens
gently; pints line up on Murray's wall;

Elaine, like me, doesn't like being shushed:
singermen, sinnermen, w/ever.
She can do the dead man's float forever.
Pauline really likes blue cheese.
Nashville can't remember its past,
Joel from Nova Scotia tells us; while Memphis
can't forget it.
        Meantime, from a ship
of rubbish & tobacco, the story of the Dutchman
fascinates the Finn:
gone full Bofin
"Coastal navigation
gets its claws into your back"
she's retweeting, & another singer
makes the beagle in the aisle fall asleep.
        The dog steals the show, but Elaine
can do the dead man's float
forever, while the session's going on.
Blue cheese Pauline has a birthday brownie,
one candle in it; what am I doing with that
lighter, if I don't smoke?
        If we burnt something
(the dead man's) by the cliffside
(float forever), we're not at liberty to disclose.
        Kit 'Pussy' Townsend dances with a bear,
armpits winking; the venusian east beach
too fucking hot.
Anne-Sofia's going full coastal navigation,
threatening to pay
for her accommodation, or else
burn the cash at the bar of the Black Gate.
Peadar feasts & lodges us like a king.
        We're loading Bofin,
bringing Bofin to the mainland,

the big stupid box first, what next, what
next? Stop complaining, lads.
blue cheese
Cowboys, absolute cowboys.
extreme
I've double-wrapped two
scattering
prints of winedark seaweed.
bright
You are always singing to yourself...

FIDDLEHEADS
for Rina Kikuchi

Mount Fuji. I'm at her feet
but maybe shan't see her –
In the best seat, should mists part,
the E seat, the bullet train's best chance –
Then, I do.
The venerable scholar
unfolded a red paper wrapper
with a dissatisfied air,
uncapped a red-ink pen
to draw with a fine nib
the erotic Fallopian tube of a fern.
This, to illustrate what he had not meant.
His friend, the young Ulsterman, misunderstood,
on their journey to the deep North
and into deep drinking; and made it lovelier,
about the body.
In fact, it had been about criticism,
how the softer structures
have given way to something dry and hard.
Time to review notes
and translations.
At a certain age, a century,
humans become unhuman, as do cats.
Cats at a certain age upgrade to being demons.
(We did not mean to witness
the prince of darkness in a fiery cloak,
hauling himself to birth behind the bar, ~
walking backwards and inverted, buttocks upward,
arms pressed into service as dissected-lily feet;
nor his opening out again to smash the stage.)
The pronunciation of cicada

cannot be agreed, though their song
can be stylized.
(We did mean to meet the poets who are not dead,
breakfast on green chrysanthemums, dine on literal roses,
and we did.)
For once, it is not an ocean,
nor one of my misreadings,
terroir / terreur, blue / blur.
She discloses herself. I do believe.
Mount Fuji. We speed by at her feet.

A WORKING BREAKFAST

Lydia's tiger worms cohabit in relative silence:
nibbing, narrowing, rubbing, coalescing,
vermilion wormbodies, sometimes lone,
cohabit in peelings; tiger worms, unsleeping,
liquid wormets of hopes and tappings.
Kitchen digested to garden, horsemen redressed in a kilim,
worms' undreamt audience dispensing endless blue-sky, endless
lavender, Iraqi figurative endless piece of birds –
The sea is warm, the earth is warm, the air bites its own tail,
n'a rien à dire, starts the infinite, applies day as a finish,
summer as a farmer's dream – two peacocks fly away,
flying back multiplied –
friend, friend in relative silence,
pleasecomeflying.

Prayer lurks in the uncertain air between poetry and philosophy, in the heat at the coppery base of the cezve, in the steam of the human breath meeting the haar of a northern morning where the sun rises orange over a bitter sea.

Witness this endeavour of faith in the poet Helen and the philosopher Aaron's Leeds coffee-house conversational book project. Additionally witness the accompanying assertions of faith, such as the faith in almonds, and the acts of faith accompanying these additional assertions of faith. Witness the extension of faith to California, a land whose existence remains unproven to me by experience: California also of oranges and salt water, California of wildfires, California of sequoias, California producer of eighty per cent of the world's almonds, a land of silica mines, fistfuls of protein, and air miles.

Prayer lurks in the agon of poetry and philosophy. Rejoice therefore, as if divinely caffeinated. Rejoice even in the side effects. Rejoice in the used grounds. Hosanna from the straw men of argument, rising like a struggle and reduced to streamers. Hosanna from the organs in subtle states of damage from false yoga, felt and undetected, hot, compressed, suffered, diagnosed. Hosanna from the souls of the insects and minerals crushed to make paint for gaudy Greek and Roman statues, before those icons were whitened for much later museums into the likeness of whitened cemeteries for much later colonizers' great wars.

Prayer lurks in the exalted origins of coffee on our originator continent; in the upraising of Yemen and the grandeur of Yemen's port of Mocha, original exporter of the brilliant beans and lender of its rich name to our lower-case blend named mocha; in the upraising of the intoxicating civilization of Ethiopia; the upraising of the sophisticated thirst of Egypt. Raise up these primary hosts of the world's coffee-houses. Praise to their early enliveners. Praise to the Sufi mystics, frequenters of the coffee-houses. Praise praise praise to the unnumbered branches and unusual grounds of their debates. Praise to the acerbic throat of the great grey wolf, the Ottoman Empire, popularizer of coffee to its tiny kittycat rival, Venice, Venice who played catchup by opening its own café in 1647, the first in the west.

Rest in blessed memory, Jacob, called 'the Jew' by an English diarist. Delurk from history how the newness of Jacob's business was also a return, three hundred and sixty years after the king expelled all Jews from England. Live, readers and coffee-drinkers, and think to praise the good taste of the modern-minded Jacob; hot on the heels of the Venetians, he opened England's first coffee-house, in 1651, in Oxford, that city where the learned reputedly talk and profess.

OUTPOURING

After Zoë Skoulding, Footnotes to Water

rivers that are rivers are driven not to stay rivers
news of rivers stays new rivers decay decaying rivers renew
rivers are history launderers rivers are mystery laundresses
rivers are misty corporations rivers are mossy incorporeal
rivers migratory homebodies gush out from the bedside drawer
in every motel in multiple translation filling the room
taking the window out spendy in every currency
and the mind back to the gutter and the gutter back to the mine
and the mine back to coal to diamond and the miner back to immortal
in a blink
        or a murmur
              or an ignorable transcendent infrasong
eyelashes wilful refusals
        to border delimit cover
              glistening candour of eyeballs
efface a face reveal a skull
        beneath the bone the brain within
              water again rills of water

pedestrian rivers	real plagues
somnambulant rivers	real sheep
imaginary rivers	real floods
innumerable rivers	real code
commercial rivers	real death
unaccustomed rivers	real shift
phantasmal rivers	real heat
collaborative rivers	real heft
incontestable rivers	real sheep
unmappable rivers	even more real sheep
Adda the river	Zoë the skald:

: *Tell me tell me tell me tell me*
Bluebell to Body ~ Body to Bury ~

Eel to Elephant ~ Meme to Moiré ~
Odd volumes ~ Pleistocene to Pond ~
Skatepark to Stickleback ~ Teint to Tongue ~
Uncollected to Untranslated ~ Erratum slip ~
English to water ~ French to water ~
Lyric to water ~ Stepped lines to water ~
A stumbling block to water ~ Typeface to water ~
Water to Welsh ~ Water to wet.
Wet to wired. Wring and rinse,
so the Victorian bird sang;
so the later birds censored.
Waving to drowning. Today to eternity.
Mirror to river. River to face.
O there are stories of things looked at,
loved, lost, forgotten, dug up, washed out,
catalogued, pissed upon, the scarlet woman,
lamplit, the nurse, houses, the incredible
numerical erosion by houses, houses,
the incredible unhabited reflection of houses,
a whisper of work, a whisper of a force
at work that is not work, nature, labour,
the nature of labour, labouring nature,
every route a river ghost, and we are
in it, fearfully, we are of it,
wonderfully, mud, I see through you,
clear as mud, written into the Book of Zoë,
larval, metamorphosing, mud coming
of mud, nothing could be clearer,
no thing could be, clearer…

ACCURACY
After William Empson, 'Aubade' (1937)

Hours

could take

up

large
buildings

The guarded

rest
the best thing

The language
for lying

KISSING DISTANCE

The rain it raineth every day
also stylle as dew in Aprille
the quality of mercy
The rain it raineth every day
They will welcome him forcefully
O temps suspend ton vol
The rain it raineth every day
also stylle as dew in Aprille

The rain it raineth every day
Your company my starvation
Every leaf speaks bliss to me
The rain it raineth every day
Dew in Aprille fallyt on the spray
and I in my bed again
The rain it raineth every day
Your company my starvation

The rain it raineth every day
Gloria in excelsis
Earth sweetens sailors for the sea
The rain it raineth every day
Praise death no-one can run away
to die upon a kiss
The rain it raineth every day
Gloria in excelsis

& they turned up the cards –
the soy candle snickered –
something clicked; they said,
let's call her up, a dream
of frail girls; genetic
sexual attraction –
place your hand, your hand, your –
flatly; hold a séance
       the stones spoke owls;
       the owls spoke walls;
       the walls spoke moss;
       the moss spoke most –
of nothing;
       of frail girls.
COMING THROUGH
       Stoner Dee in denim shorts,
       heavy on the eyeliner,
       shooting Andy Warhol first
NOT HER!
       French-film, traffic-jam Doro
       hits up Ellis Bell, deserts
       her car, heads into the woods
ARE YOU THERE?
       Frail girl, faint girl, violet,
       between-the-liner, support
       act, sister, let's rescue you!
WHAT
       Have we raised? In a top hat?
       Drawling, "Call me Desmond. Come
       to the cabaret"? & they

dropped the cards
put out the lights
stopped the clocks
declared her dead
picked a bowl
of daffodils,
unnerved by her
bodiful, double-rainbow laughter

SHE WANTS A FIRE, EVEN IN THE SUMMER
for Polly Atkin

Sometimes a road is a major event.
A walk endures more than a calendar.

April January February March
Chest full of bluebells, breath a wet black bough.

March, March, marriage to a stage magician
Spring, again you love sawing me in half.

Coughing up fur balls, a wealth of wool, May
Rewilds me; foaming, I mouth May, a wolf.

Summer bestows few vows; December comes
As June's bare effigy; a month, a tooth,

Falls out; jaws of the year breathing bluebells,
Giblet pies. I can write, or talk. Not both.

Should July have held hands with September?
August overdosed on June? Sun enough

In my marrow for wet stockings to do
For entire weeks of June; each breath

A word chesting up from the inky desk
Of heaviness; October was one month

Or three, I tell you; November, a road.
My feet set down December. Crip time's betrothed.

ECOLOGIES OF ATTENTION
for Alice Tarbuck

a table made of applewood
an apple grows at home
a woodland cored to press a fence
upon the apple's home
a dance of seeds around the core
a round to dance alone
by heart you know the steps like men
like bears who sleep alone

see a storm, be in the storm, or stop
the storm: an act of will
stops the storm? in imitation
of a storm stopping by an act
not of will, if weather had will,
your will imitating the storm's
flash of recognition: lightning
does not stop, makes eerie darkness
lightning that does not stop, stops, starts,
love, biting like love, more than like

i mouth slepe
   lik grasse stalkes
   lik querewolves
   softe neckes
pterodactyl neighbourhoods
   preen endure
   toebean hazards
   dinocure

editor! they're on
the world stage!

laughing! and dancing!
when you know!
their body language!
should be pain!
cotton! cobblestone! pain!
editor! they're speaking!
editorially! again! stopstop
good good pay
sob reproduce lawsuit
inscape gratitude outrage

lik holi thing
groaning aloft
an innocent
attention lapse
ecologies
of thistledown
neolithic
somnambulism

anyway we are sitting on one washed rock
  together
                for the indefinite
                              let's talk
where   from
place   forgetting
place   forgetfulness
place   would forget

are you
fistful   blood
library   armies
conflagration   bedrooms
piss-cup   precious stones

wherefrom midnight
lunar lastday
calendar   knocking
knocking the base of one of the statues

the plinth will open and
tell

they cannot   build
they   find
their echo chamber
the open sky

interesting! borrow a
rose garden! most
interesting! drum up
an adequate cohort
of toads! well

is
   who
indigenous to horseback
is
   who
indigenous to airports
is
   who
native to swimming pools
is
   who
native to deserts
is originally
appropriation
is originally

the longest queue
ancestry
  strangers
ancestry
  embers
ancestry
  labourers
ancestry
  lawyers
ancestry
  mobsters
beggars piemakers
beautiful beggars
unpublished piemakers
priests on repeat
bridegrooms who make up their face
the fair and the fierce
the sun and the moon
sharing
a ring

anyway we are leaning in
      on one washed rock
together for the indefinite
                   rise

by heart you know the steps like lace:
: a willingly pierced face

SCALES OF LOSS AND LONGING

I walked to the lighthouse with you
all of you who are absent
and I said
>   the face of the moon
>   soon would be ploughed up
and you said
conscious of the queen of heaven
>   the moon doesn't have a face
and I said to you
presently
>   the moon would be furrowed
>   in a way you could see from earth
and then we looked
half absently
at the ruby cloud ingathering
and the tactless moon
>   encroached upon us
>   endeared itself to us
>   displaced in time from us
>   exploitable in names like ours
and I said
exactly because you aren't here
walking past the old chained pier
which is shut
and are you hurrying
into a sleepy pleat
I said
>   when I can't see
>   I hear
the lift in your voice
>   when I can't hear
>   I feel

the lift in your form
              when I can't feel
              I sense
the lift in your heart
I say it walking with you
when you
absent
perhaps not walking
reply
                   the face
                   the lighthouse
                   some harmony
                   the moon

COMMEDIA

Mr Alighieri, I'm curious.
Who cleaned your shoes, when you got back from hell?
What brand are they? And how hard are your soles?
You stampeded through the bitter wanwood;
at least a twig, if not a yellow flower
must've stuck. You were super unsure
about your footing. That's why you give us
instructions how to steady our feet.
I wonder. Sometimes, on your way, you fell
asleep. I understand you slept in hell.
I've almost done that. With your drastic drop-
and-pass-out, you're like someone taking cover
from natural catastrophes: drop and hold on.
The good interpreters come pigeoning.
They nod: *that sleep's a trance; that one's a rapture;*
this time, he's in celestial ecstasy…
No, no! Even in hell, you were being
repaired. Did a bluesilver angel bend
lower than earthward, feathering footwear
smooth and clean for you? Did the temperature
changes help with the dirt? Steam-treatment
in the adulterers' swirl? An ice rinse later?
Anyway, you stepped up. Saw the stars again.
You're saved. So you don't have a ghost. That sigh
at my shopping-mall anxiety
is Vergil's shade, perhaps, kit list in hand
summed up in one word: FOLLOW. You swapped out
that list for one word: LOVE. I want to know,
Mr Alighieri, who cleaned your shoes?
And which nameless guest forgot his jacket
in my pinewood wardrobe? Many people
stayed while I was away. I'm wearing it.
Scarlet leaves are crawling from my pockets.

BLACK ICE

these nights the ice melts   but the ice is not melting   these nights it has been raining overnight   but the ice is not melting   these nights the ice melts   but the dawn refreezes the streets   not melting   ice please shine please spangle   this ice very does not

ice   and staircase becomes a failing   spine and spangle   something moves   staircase is a falling   noctilucent piano keys   loose teeth   sardinian cheese walking   as living a feeling of falling   staircase to failing   these nights honeycomb   laying down   a glaze   I gaze from several angles   the ice melts   but is not melting   even here   black means invisible

DREAM OF A, DREAM OF

The pale horse entered houses
wanting to be watered, fed,
not staying where you led it
and when you found it again
cornered you in the kitchen
up against the sink and bit
you
the pale horse from that book

Common ungarden flowers milktooth and pinking shear their gaudy
   weird to ground.
Tell me you've never counted them. Tell them you've never counted.
Times out of number, hot little series win, a flower falling under its
   components
or falling under ombre attachment. Flowing pity? No, a dry little beaker,
so tell her any such flung thing, the past, is an unflowing part.
Madrugada. Iris. Checked, it checks out, courting peace from your
   permitted list.
Perfume, snowglobes, mascara, tape, glass, tapestry, glassestry, pastry, a
   contrapart.
Will you call it the pull of the moon when it is the bruise within the limb
between the violet & green call it between the violet & concrete
weathered into all the pretty horsefaces? Is the door alarmed enough?
Is the door between floors? Are the floors parquetry or honey?
Do ice skates travel over floorboards? Do white spaces take on airs
of woodland? Does woodland take the air with springtime?
Shuttle clean into peaceable unsleep. Identity dreams in bar codes,
death before or after or as a form of spring, star-softening, unanimous
   laughter,
doxxed speech, sweet hiss of curriculum vitæ, tuberose bathroom

occupation, parched grass, a chronic foam of comradeship hedging
bullyship, iron-on badges take a freezeover beneath mackerel skies
over the lackless sea at twenty-seven thousand feet, twenty-seven thousand
yesterdays, twenty-seven thousand purple dawns. Resurrect, never a gun
   in sight.
Clouds look into incorporation of underblue, honeycomb romance soup.
GAUDEIX de bridges of iris, that cannot be played back. Springtime:
discalced. A scaly-footed bird, wading out of water, walks on
the grass, finding itself unshod; feathered with roses; a tender arc blowing
in the small print.

DUST AND PROUD OF IT

Death is no secret thing
Does not come visiting
Already in the room
Makes us at home
Death's pronoun is not It
Oats neither spilt nor split
Corner the purpling mouth
Spider for moth
Some take hands some turn backs
Or purify or tax
Relationships they hold
While uncontrolled
Death will not organize
Placard or canonize
Or more than seem to choose
Doors we can't close

PURPLE

miss you from wherever you've gone
and you make a habit of going
as if departure were a texture
wool   rope   oil   water
and you a haute couture collagist
had to try them all
an embarrassment of amethysts
a rental of incandescence
a portcullis of contracts
a tall ship of suggestibility
an unconsciousness of exclusion
an inclusion of unconsciousness
an editorial of thunder and lightning
a staple of staples
a small word in the air

IT TRANSPIRES

trees are not women
dramatic representation
may make them witness
alongside Castle Terrible
monsterproportionate to events
those who can uproot
splintsplaining elmish panels
plainer than trees they model
shapes that do not tell
of breath
shapes that do
not tell

COERCION BANQUET

i say don't forage mushrooms
at all   the dark woods they say
are uncool   but thank you thank
you and we refuse to   know
pure mourning is happening
ideologically
pure mourning   a mushroom ring
righteous trespass docs
crocs and sandals up some field
you don't look like you feel   and
am I that name   is it grass
grass or glass   eat   what   they
show me rag idolatry
a lying grasp at nettles
mindful fracturation cards
another   show me the way

POINT OF IMPACT

percussion marks   fine scars
struck flint's   visible voicing
mobile phone's   tactile evolution
reverting to handaxe   glossy handset
smooth to pleasure   the throwing hand
smart prehistories   stored in stone

what of the rock I licked
and wrote with, wrongly,
in the workshop – dabbing
its millions-old neb on paper,
mudstone resoftened to mud
and millions-old tunnelled wormhole

...

it can be mild when it gets you
small fowl overflown by falcon shadow
firedrakes overflying Northumbria
couldn't you tell without being told

a thunderstorm puts out the power
the water doesn't stop when lightning strikes
as you put your hand out to the metal
can't budge while voltage runs through you

...

you are as weak as water
and somehow still alive
little girl at home
called little boy by strangers

the wooden chair larger than yourself
little boy called little girl
at home by strangers
voicebox blue with vocal fry

Can this mild waterfall be called
      a waterfall at all? I follow
           clear water flowing over rock
broadening into stairs of water
      flowing over rocks, broadening
           to seating-places, limestone-mild;
knowing there are tripping-places,
      drowning-places, I sit softly
           in flowing water listening
to people singing, walking hard.
      I, who never had the talent
           to improvise, sing a descant.
You were there, friend. And you were there
      in the swimming baths, where ladies
           talked of hip and knee replacements.
You were there, a flash of fuchsia
      when my eyes blacked out, but I kept
           talking till bullying unlooped.
A soft and tricky sacrifice
      phosphoresces up from marshland.
      You are there. You maze me away.
Mountain descending a staircase,
      you appear all plateaus, promise
           amazement, if only
I can stop seeing upside-down,
      seeing everything upside-down.
           Do you want to talk? Here I am.

MEANWHILE, CICADAS

If we take
all the fish
out the lake
once a year,
if we check
for native fish
against invasive fish,
if we put
invasive fish in
special boxes, put
native fish back
in the lake,
if we take
good care, use
pure detergents, soap–
free soap, perhaps
the lake will
from its dark
rough clear north
to its green
choppy south be
good to us,
livable, never gentle,
never yet measured,
not cause drowning,
drought, not be
cross, or crossed.

STILL, STILL

Hold your arm like a branch,
swaying from the shoulder
solid in a balance
a sitting hawk may trust.
Number the thirteen ducks,
fed with appropriate
proteins, none of your bread,
maybe peanut butter.
Think on such things while you
wait, while they fail to raise
a vein, when the raised vein
is childsize, when they save
on equipment, and won't
change needles. Hold your arm.

PERFUME HOWL
for Tiffany Atkinson

true ectomorphs walk among us
arcades of ectomorphs   scintillæ
cavalcades of ectomorphs   streetlamps
fusillades of ectomorphs   shotguns
calvaries of ectomorphs   scanners
an aeroplane walked among us
gabbling crucifixion
it came from another better land
I took you by the hand
Madam I would not trifle
with you   would you care
for a bit of bitter geranium
spritz the air walk into the Missed
the drydown is an ectomorph
it raises a pine a pine a pine
O in these undogly times
in this undogly situation
beleaguered by ectomorphs
in this undogly nation
hallow

      cry

            hallow
adored familiar howl

RHYTHM

After Sir Philip Sidney, Astrophil and Stella *31*

Wth hw sd stps (i, uh, aaah)
      O MOON ...
Hw slntl... hw wn... !
Wht   tht
tht   rch sh rp rrws
       O   O
   O   O   O
      OO
   ee
       O MOON
constantlovewantofwitconstantlovewant
ofwitconstantlovewantofwitconstant

   rubies   red   you   mine   be   here
are beauties proud? are beauties proud? here. be.

are   you above love? the fisherman waits
above love be lov'd and yet

   stiltwalkers exact vengeance firemen dance on ladders
o lovers scorn o love o possess

ohhh ah uh you air uh
         ffff
        FULLlllness

THEY DON'T NEED TO BREAK

Who saw centipedes, thought they had seen grass   **A thought is twisting up:**

rise like brown twine   **this leafy glade isn't one to lay your cheek against.**

out of mounded green grass? who fails   the trees are hot. they were shot for that

to check the holes about their feet   film of paradise. emerald hearts swapped

fails to respect how reptiles fill out lean grass.   out. apples of eyes cut

which mighty cobra scorns an ants'-nest   to reveal

home set ready-made for coiling in   a dancing

the lean grass?   star.

an earthworm, parched and desperate,   you could refresh

may route   yourself in the dark, you could drink

through gutters;   blood

dry blades stand for what had been   from branches.

grass. sun,

lovelier than fire, playing   go forward, more than halfway. they don't   or

sharp, draws unseen   **need to break** for you. they don't need to break

seeds to ripe next level sheen grass.   to speak. they need to speak.

FAULT LINES

Ai ai ai ai ai – Ohé ohé –
Ai ai – Ohé – Hey –
Hello, sailor, ha ha
Come ashore –
Green gumboots,
green green dollars,
green hello, hey you –
The horizon's up-tipped
like a buttercup-chin
tintinnabulant citrine
hymns of ecstasy –
Bless this latitude,
its underwater defences,
industrial-strength bells,
hunger song loafing about –
Put fish right back
as climate might have left them
in clover
quando cœli movendi sunt et terra –
Ai ai ai ai – Ohé ohé –
green words –

PUT OUT THE LIGHT
for Johsua Lue Chee Kong

hold on to your handkerchiefs
especially embroidered
i misremembered it
as after the earthquake
he 3D-printed
the cathedral for a headpiece
to play his mas
but no
it was after
commercial demolition
partially accomplished
of anti-slavery Greyfriars
Trinidad's landmark
the masquerader handcrafted
a model Greyfriars
to midnight his protest
in festival sun
i misremembered how
this guy carried
church on his head
it literally happened
they appointed judges
who awarded points
Christ have mercy
who was among them
nobody
I myself

BRASS FACE

were several instruments installed
mistakenly as externals
payless in bodily airways
ventilated petitioner
of ecstatic unions is it
) punctuation light (
safe to say seems sound to say so

PARADISO: YOU'RE SUCH A CHILD!

Oh no, oh yes. There's that one
who loves the rollercoaster.
You're passed out on a bench; she's having fun.
Oh no, oh yes. There's that one
laughing and begging: *Let's go back on?*
She lives life like life itself; you couldn't ghost her.
Oh no, oh yes. There's that one
who loves the rollercoaster.

My tiny hippopotamus, bandog, or lost species, was not mislabelled as a ritual object, unlike the broken combs, cosmetic jars, and other inexplicable mystery discards tweezered from their floodplain or festival-skirted magma tombs. It was labelled as a toy. But for four thousand years nobody has played with it. And when the woman knocked at your side door in the house with no front door, you skinned her with one glance and saw you were one blood, you and she, but her people earliest had left the floodplain and the festival-skirted magma tombs where yours wintered and mantraed, deserting much longer after. Much longer after every each day and after the day tomorrow. That is how it is counted. I am six years old plus four and a half thousand years. When she quickly changed the price of her cloth wares and refused to cross your threshold, there were no more toys, only glass, glass for a few thousand years. Your notes danced in her hand and she despised you in her heart. But my reddy-orange toy, which has a happy face, is looking up. I don't mind if you break it. Don't worry about anything. Don't worry. Let's play.

WITHOUT ARMOUR

A race is happening across the field. Its course involves caravans, horses, three kingqueens, real camels, linen & bleached canvas. Did I come out without my armour?

A race is happening. Someone in white, attached by his heels, dragged by a chariot, half on the ground, body and robes pulled along, looks full-face towards us.

He is laughing. Is this a violence? And part of the race? Winner in white, in the thick of the crowd, he laughs as if dragged and winning.

They are laughing with him.

He is on his feet, an El Greco crescent; down again, an El Bosco fluorescent.

What is this race? Small amounts of thyme enter everywhere, small
   amounts of thyme everywhere, rosewood answers.

WHATEVER YOU'RE DOING

STOP
      when the stranger arrives,
give them lime juice,
something cold to drink,
somewhere to ease
their probably filthy feet
KNOW
      you internalize many such sayings,
      as your ceiling must internalize moths,
      cobwebs, stainblossom,
      and immortelle seed

SPACE

After William Empson, 'Aubade' (1937)

standing

deaths

bawl

.

blank

you   have seen   a

heart

OF SILENCES

holy is the protocol:
sitting in a discard   dressed up as a cinder
all-consumed particulate   glowing to fail apart
holy is the shoulderbag   holy the shoelaces
holy the brutal perpetrator of piercing light
daytime discards butoh dancers
calendared in clingfilm   atheists towards day
clingfilm peels   off one self
costumed in fatigues   watering the air
tabled taffeta walking a wake
Orson Welles' Othello's
extra O gulfed between
'the cause' and 'my soul'
holy is the cortisol   holy the lactic acid
holy the non-steroidal anti-inflammatory legal drugs
clingfilm peels   off a second self
couches prop up   sloughed cocoons
someone multiplied   not I myself
holy the…
sitting in a discard   a wordless cry
after more light   more air
here am I able to rise and cross   rise up and cross
cross over
over to the other side of quite
quite a small space
holy the integument   holy the cut-price hospital gauze
holy the process of reverse mummification
holy the…
daytime   I am…
or somebody is… yearning
O

promise us an ocean
with top-notch dolphins
whose shiny bellies rival
any moon of platinum love,
crescent bodies incredible,
leaping with the force that is like joy,
forceful and leaping for joy

HE / THEY

they walk to the edge of the pier
        two fools
he inks five words on a padlock
        hopeful thankful
he fastens the lock to the wire
        distressful regretful
he turns back he walks on further
        wildering recallable
the tide comes in saying remember
        perfected indelible
the sea remembers you in its prayers
        sentimental untenable
the lighthouse a tower of rainbow
        resurrectionary inalienable
what good is this
        ?
the harbour is doomed to go under
        not the harbour the supermarket
amen   love

GENTLE HOUSEWORK OF THE SACRIFICE

PROFESSION

Annunciation hormone
'relaxin' what's relaxing when
relaxin'll reconfigure your bones

by unbinding all your sinews
throughout pregnancy never the same
rebinding never the same again

metanoia
child's play to this
blue sky sky blue ripping

birther of nothing
I will pick up my sword
the one I gave away

Mother Francis
I swear by my chromosomes
I'll be a decent brother xx

CHOSEN FAMILY
for Josie Giles

At the table

my name in your mouth is

                    appalling

my name in your mouth is

                    exceptional

my name in your mouth is

                    overwhelm

my name in your mouth is

                    you

and my name in your mouth is

                    why

why why

In the living room

a hole no bigger than a pencil
than my snappiest fingerbone
and the darling   the snub and corny
darling   never a word expected
gone.
      we find our kindness   our children
our warm sand company   our best strange
at the littlest scale of living
things that think unlike our most loving.
floorboards   like muscovado sugar
melt. and stick. and sweep. and burn. like tears
in rope   someone else was holding. gone.

And then they realized

[   ] is like
is
like a room when the moment when
the forbidden terrier
jumps reckless of injury
opens the door at a silent rush
bedside   kneels up folds paws
turns a stern eye on the feverish patient
and the ghost of the dirty-faced heedless boy
and the work-pale girl who does not mean well

[   ] is like
is
like a family when the time when
the ingenious labrador
races into the car
dangling the pit viper he caught
live   as a gift
and delighted by the shrieking
brings more and more
activity snakes to his pack

[   ] is like
is
like a road when like the winter when
the molossive pupper
herds the determinedly solitary walker
happily
to be even more happily
unnecessarily
saved
in the snow

MIGRAINE IMPROV
for Nat Raha

as big as you can
as small as you can
make it the same thing
  seagull on the roof
  common snipe in the yard
  24/7 birdsound
wet feather
white flutter
floodwater
  volcano blackout
  volcano privilege
  volcano print
distant volcano
extinct volcano
volcano voile
  paper recycling
  fly away Peter
  fly away Paul
suffer
sulphur
soufflé
  snowflakes syringes
  bananas oranges
  statisticians foragers
mask no mask
nose mask mask
ventilator ventilation
  dense lesbian trees
  marriageable parasol geraniums
  abandoned lighthouse

dense lesbian trees
people fall on their faces
things are looking up
dense lesbian trees
sweet singing in the choir
sweet singing in the choir

"DOON YER TEA, EAT YER BREAD"

A faint resentment paints
the spiral staircase walls
blue all over again,
unheimlich as a school
bazaar, as gilded eggs,
as rebonding plaster.
Footsteps. Stop one floor down.
Is that too soon. Or not.
They aren't yours? Colour this
now, collect it like likes,
call it no name, no name.
I have seen the best minds
of my generation
turned into deer. About
time, too. Fuck resonance.
Streetside, virus baubles
the heatstroke jetty air.
Lyric! Cannae come in.
Vampiric lyric, you're
banished. O my threshold,
my threshold, threshing floor
and sea floor, loud as foil.
O my deer, my hamlet,
my flowering wall, O
ladder to breakages,
nightmare's gown, summoning
moonvowels. *Exeunt.*
I will go out. I will
Breathe. Breath is the spirit.
When's a door not a door?
Too many empty rooms.

YOUTH

every each day best
bring up the girl without pink
says princess daddy
eat rhoticity chicken
resist transgressive dickery

WHITE EGRETS

Change this wherever-I-am
to a playground so I can
run away run pointlessly
away in a wide open
playground shouting I hate you
I hate you I hate you and
let the sobbing begin my
sobbing as you stand any-
where and everywhere you can
see and hear me anyway
and I think you're not crying
and I think you're not even
impressed and the quartz piles up
the chalk and limestone gravel
we're under renovation
love in this stumbling school

I IS A PRONOUN

Hear her relax release
grammar case by case
like dressage like a dressing
like a dismount like a mountain
like a tourniquet like a ticket
tossed into, sunlit-perfect,
the high throat of a non-combustible bin.
Hem him wired withered
like a horse's tail like silver tinsel
like a salon floor like ashes
like a sequence like a challenge
in the grassy selving syntax
of a Roman road, direct, no
longer taken. Ai my
love, this is none of us.
A plague of visitors upon this place.
A ring of lucifers upon this flyer.
A famine of genders upon these permissions.
A mean of colours upon this slip.

HOT SPRINGS DISSOCIATION

The window when I can do things
is very small.
The auxiliaries it lights up
drink, bet and brawl.
Lilac, amber, lapis lazuli
light up their dreams.
I look for another century.
They game and steam.

MIKE, SWIMMING

for C. Michael Chin

I am convinced my body
wants to be free of its breasts
and   bleeding or not   to fly
with imaginable joy
unimaginable pain
flexing   not as the angels
but as cathedrals do   stone
through which light is expressed
and just as clouds shift   shift shape
shed rain   creating blue shade
waking seeds and illusions.
I swim devastating lengths
turning again   not to meet
myself   O my companions
in silence   but to break breath
with shimmering you   destroyed
into lifegiving droplets
cupped heads a tumult of shine.
I know you by immersion
shared gasps   not by your faces
neither concealed nor revealed
loving beyond bodyshame
as above   so below   so
sky and water pool in one
and never the same motion.
My body is new with joy.

THE SUMMER IS HOTTER

shock is writ in splash
splash is writ in water
water in a river
river writ in shock in splash
in first encounter
encounter :: otter
otter and water always
the first as water is
always new river
otter always new otter

IMAGINARY GARDENS
for Sarah Cave

war! after silence
labyrinth! for the allotment
peppermint! in the hot stone
bonxies! at the sea's edge
shriek! in the orchard
hogs! with intact ears and tails
a pail of corpse-fish
a pail of compost-sugar
a good knockdown argument
at the altar rail
your church is covered with ramblers
roses mushrooming rucksacks
unchecked   bringing gifts of
subtraction
long have I waited
I am ten times the man
of any man or woman of you
without having to do anything
about it
when we are far away
far enough
one of us   becomes the world
the other   discoverable
are you ok with the spaces
                in this
will they be   able to
download the downloadable
is   the programme
too hungry
        too
                slow

NEVER HAVE I EVER

I've been bending the ear of God
for years, sure and impermanent
as rust water saddens the dyes
pressed from buddleia leaves and grass
on rags nobody thought to hem
before cutting, and now I do
think of it; won't do it though
when you tell me to stop praying
for you you're saying stop something
I can't help. All neighbourhoods need
a Utility Queer but I
never was a dab hand with a
toolbox. I'll kick any bucket.
Take away my prayer, make me the
Neighbourhood Futility Queer.
Teach me how to swear to the end
of the breakwater, in Polish,
and all the way back, in Greek. I'll
tell you the one about the bear
I heard in Ireland. Bonfires
on the beach. Secondary smoke…
Mari Juana, herb of wisdom,
clinging to the clifftop cyclist.
You've never done illegal drugs?
Too many killings. Hear my prayer.

Believing   that dogs will go to heaven
  (there will be dogs in heaven)
Wanting   all the dogs in heaven
  (there will be dogs in heaven)
Not leaving   enough dogs for other people in heaven
  (there will be dogs in heaven)

SMOL THING ATTE PLAY

it exists

daffodils are higher than my toes
dandelions higher than my nose
yet I am not buried
what am I?
very smol
on ane hill

it seeks .

source of song
snug and bite
boing and flink
flump and fight
is there one pool
where you are all
that swims
that blinks
that hunts
that calls?

it hides

human offering
wildflowers
in eggcups
to look at
been stopped
while alive
smol thing

has eaten
yellow off walls
licked the stone
likes to remain
buttery
uncollected

The sacrifice got up off the altar.
BECOME AN ARCHAEOLOGIST OF YOUR LUNGS.
      Windrush
is the name of a ship
not of a generation
      Windrush
is the name of a ship
not of any situation
      Windrush
is the witchcraft name of a ship
waterlining us into uncharted, obligatory, and perpetual migration

The sacrifice got up off the altar.
BECOME AN ARCHAEOLOGIST OF YOUR LUNGS.

The naming of ships is a terrible thing,
The Terrible Mother tell me.

I came in a ship called
      Threat Vector
I came in a ship called
      Dust to Dust
Who came in a ship called
      Willing Ambassador
Who came in a ship called
      Evidence of Funds
Did I dance with you on the blue carpet?
Was your ship called the Providence?
The Invitation? Was your ship called Guerilla Diplomacy?

Go back where you came from, citizens,
Says Terrible Motherland,
whether that means overseas
or going back under the sea,
citizens, life forms.
Listen to the lady, she is a consultant anonymizer,
A high-mobility native of Fortress Trolley.
We are phantasmagorically, primarily, and politically
lightless and all-bearing creatures
put down, not undrowned, gone beyond
beyond drowned

The sacrifice got up off the altar.
BECOME AN ARCHAEOLOGIST OF YOUR LUNGS.

A woman is sweeping the sea.
In the father's words, in Kamau's words,
a woman is sweeping the sea.
They still say in English
a ship is a 'she'?
Who say so? The ship is
a thing of itness
witness and creator
fury of a wake
raking over of witness
The island scholar is sweeping the carpet
in her London digs
sweeping the sea-grey, the pea-souper carpet
in no-blacks no-Irish no-dogs London's aspirational digs
that carpet had etiquette, it demanded her to accept it
in its misty itness, as grey, grey like ethical practice, dove-or-pigeon grey.
Could the island scholar
trust loose-talking fibre
after she study the French liberator

Charles de Gaulle
Who dismissed our archipelago
as specks of dust?
She sweeps and a pattern emerges
stabilizing as many colours
stabilizing as a miracle
a many-coloured pattern wanting to dance beside her feet
after she was forced to breathe in dust
settling and unsettling
the miracle of many colours

The sacrifice got up off the altar.
BECOME AN ARCHAEOLOGIST OF YOUR LUNGS.

ACKNOWLEDGEMENTS

'Summer, Launceston' was commissioned by the Charles Causley Trust for the reopening of Launceston Castle, Cornwall (2022).

'Full-Circle Bells' was written for Dr Sarah Jackson's AHRC-funded project, *Crossed Lines: Literature and Telephony* (2019-2020).

'Weather Systems' was a contribution to *Caroline Bergvall's Medievalist Poetics: Migratory Texts and Transhistoric Methods* (Arc Humanities Press).

'Fiddleheads', 'Accuracy', 'Meanwhile: Cicadas', 'Rhythm', 'Space', 'Steal This', 'Youth', 'I is a Pronoun' are reworkings of a contribution to *Abstractions*, ed. by Paul Munden and Shane Strange (Recent Work Press, 2018). Most of these poems were drafted in the Tokyo apartment of Erica Simms Williams and Laurence Williams.

An earlier version of 'A Short Prayer to Coffee, which Crosses the Sea' appears in *Odyssey Calling* (Sad Press, 2020). It was written for the Leeds launch of Helen Mort and Aaron Meskin, *Opposite: Poems, Philosophy and Coffee* (Valley Press, 2019).

'Outpouring' responds to Zoë Skoulding's *Footnotes to Water* (Seren, 2019). It appeared in *Poetry Review*.

'Kissing Distance' was filmed for Poet in the City by the Adrian Brinkerhoff Foundation at Charles Causley's home, Cyprus Well, Launceston, by kind permission of the Charles Causley

Trust. It appeared in *Magma 84*, with a response by Maryam Hessavi, Formally, 'Kissing Distance' is both a rondeau, and a cento. Lines are from my own adaptations of Old English and of St Francis of Assisi, as well as from Middle English lyric, Emily Brontë, Alphonse de Lamartine, and William Shakespeare.

'Divining Dorothy', 'She Wants a Fire, Even in the Summer', and 'Ecologies of Attention' were commissioned by Polly Atkin for DW250 (Dorothy Wordsworth 250), and featured on the website https://dw250.uk/home/commissions/

'Scales of Loss and Longing' was written for *Out of Time: Poetry for the Climate Emergency*, ed. by Kate Simpson (Valley Press, 2021).

'Inferno: One Size Fits Most', 'Purgatorio: Thirsty Work', and 'Paradiso: You're Such A Child!' were written for *Divining Dante* (Recent Work Press, 2021), ed. by Paul Munden and Nessa O'Mahony. The anthology includes 'Purgatorio: Thirsty Work', and is freely available online https://indd.adobe.com/view/535b8362-cfa3-489d-a345-5649184ab247

'Inferno: One Size Fits Most', 'Mike, Swimming', 'Perfume Howl' and 'Never Have I Ever' appeared in *English: Journal of the English Association* (Oxford University Press, 2021.

'It Transpires' and 'Smol Thing Atte Play' appeared in *Our Time Is A Garden: New Nature Writing by Women and Nonbinary Writers of Colour*, ed. by Alycia Pirmohamed (IASH, The University of Edinburgh, 2023).

'Chosen Family' appeared in *Cordite Poetry Review* (September 2022), as 'Chosen Family Sequence'.

'Turn and Live' was written for the Royal Society of Literature 'Windrush 75 In Verse' R.A.P. Party at the London Library (2023).

Earlier versions of some much-reworked poems appear in *Poetry London* (Autumn 2018).

'A Working Breakfast', 'Profession', and 'Youth' appear online in a Mother's Day special from *anthropocene poetry*. Thanks to Lydia Wilson for inspiration and hospitality.

'Migraine Improv' and 'Doon Yer Tea, Eat Yer Bread', appear online in *Granta*.

Any errors and omissions are the fault of the author.

Thanks to numerous colleagues and fellow creatures, especially the Department of English and Related Literature at the University of York, Blackfriars Cambridge, the Charles Causley Trust, and Otto V. Atkinson.